W0463683

Technical English Basics

Lösungen
3. Auflage

VERLAG EUROPA-LEHRMITTEL • Nourney, Vollmer GmbH & Co. KG
Düsselberger Straße 23 • 42781 Haan-Gruiten
Europa-Nr.: 71969

Autoren

Bernhard Busch Hamburg
Uwe Dzeia Gleichen
Birgit Haberl Regensburg
Jürgen Köhler Northeim

Lektorat

Dr. Astrid Grote-Wolff

Das vorliegende Buch wurde auf der Grundlage der neuen amtlichen Rechtschreibregeln erstellt.

3. Auflage 2008

Druck 5 4 3 2 1

Alle Drucke derselben Auflage sind parallel einsetzbar, da sie bis auf die Behebung von Druckfehlern untereinander unverändert sind.

ISBN 978-3-8085-7198-9

http://www.europa-lehrmittel.de
Umschlaggestaltung: tiff.any GmbH, Berlin
Layout und Satz: tiff.any GmbH, 10999 Berlin
Druck: Druckerei Raimund Roth GmbH, 42655 Solingen

1 Visiting people abroad

Activity 1, page 7: Comprehension

1. LEONARDO is a language learning programme offered by the EU. It supports exchange visits of students to other countries of the EU.
2. Hanover and Bristol are twin towns.
3. Frank's hosts live in a suburb of Bristol.
4. They are training for different jobs in mechanical engineering.
5. It means you get your theoretical and practical training at different places.
6. The English students get their practical training at different firms in and around Bristol.
7. The English trainees get their theory training at a vocational college.

Activity 2, page 9: Finding information in a text

a) Bristol is situated in south-west England. It is an industrial city with about 500 000 inhabitants. It is twinned with Hanover in Germany. There are a number of modern industries in Bristol. It has a very rich history and a lot of buildings remind of Bristol's former Glory. Clifton Suspension Bridge was built by Isambard Kingdom Brunel. Bristol is also a multicultural city. There are a lot of activities and festivals in and around Bristol every year.

b) I live in a place called … It is situated about 100 km south of Hanover in Germany. … is a village in a rural area and has about 1600 inhabitants. There is no industry in our village but the surrounding area is very beautiful. Our local sports club offers a large variety of activities for young and old people. …

Activity 3, page 9: Vocabulary

1. estuary
2. inhabitants
3. base/headquarters
4. leading
5. aircraft
6. supersonic
7. suburb
8. skills
9. suspension bridge
10. constructor/engineer
11. gorge
12. steam

Activity 4, page 9: Translation

1. Bristol is a very lively industrial town in south-west England.
2. Bristol has a long history, which is closely connected to seafaring.
3. The colonies in America were supported from here.
4. Today Bristol has more than half a million inhabitants and is an important industrial city.
5. Clifton Suspension Bridge is an important building, which spans the river Avon at a height of 245 feet.

Activity 5, page 10: Answering questions

1. Mrs. Honeywell is the principal of City of Bristol College.
2. The college is the third largest in the UK. It was formed by a merger of three colleges. City of Bristol College offers a large variety of full time and part time courses.
3. It is a modern college and has excellent facilities. For example, they have modern computers and other learning equipment as well as a large library with about 50 000 books, a large number of magazines and CDs and of course PCs with full internet access.
4. The answer can't be found in the text. Individual answers.
5. Students of the Home Economics Department prepared the buffet.
6. They come together to discuss the programme for the week.

Activity 6, page 11: Answering questions

1. Eileen comes from a village near Bristol called Easter Comptom.
2. She does an NVQ course at a firm called "Click-Clock".
3. The firm produces cardboard packaging machines.
4. John Granger works at British Aerospace in Filton.
5. They have to go back to their room because they are getting some information about the programme for the week.

Activity 7, page 12: Introducing oneself

My name is .... I'am 19 years old. I live in a village about ... km south of .... I am a trainee structural mechanic with a firm called .... Once a week I attend a vocational college in .... where I get my theoretical training. I still live with my parents because I don't earn enough money to afford a flat of my own. After my training I want to study mechanical engineering at the Fachhochschule. My hobbies are playing football and breeding chicken.

Activity 8, page 12: Completing a dialogue

1. What would you like to drink?
2. Anything to eat?
3. I have.
4. I have never been to Germany.
5. Have you got/Do you have your own flat?
6. What do your parents do?
7. Have you got brothers or sisters?
8. Where do you live, Frank?
9. And have you got brothers or sisters?
10. And you? What are you going to do?
11. And where are you going to study?
12. And what about you?
13. What is that?

Activity 9, page 13: Writing a dialogue

Eileen: Frank, you told me you are training to be an industrial mechanic at VW. Can you tell me what exactly you do there?

Frank: I have to do a lot of things. As an industrial mechanic you work in maintenance and repair. Our main job is to keep the machinery in good condition. We have to do all the necessary maintenance work, or in case of a failure we have to find out what is wrong and repair it as fast as possible.

Eileen: I see, it seems to be a very responsible job.

Frank: Oh yes. And sometimes we are very busy.

Eileen: What about your home town Hildesheim, what is it like?

Frank: It's a nice town. It's not too big, but we have all the facilities you need.

Eileen: Lucky you! My home village is boring at times. Fortunately, Bristol is not too far away. At weekends I regularly meet friends there and we go to the disco together.

Frank: So you know some nice places here in Bristol. What about going out together with some people of our group? Shall we arrange something for Friday evening?

Eileen: Good idea, we can ask John and his girlfriend and some others, too. The "Louisiana" is a good place to go to. Not too expensive and not too noisy either.

Frank: Okay, let's meet there at nine p.m.

Activity 10, page 13: Writing a report

Eileen is a trainee toolmaker at "Click-clock" in Bristol. She lives together with her parents in a village near Bristol called Easter Compton. She has never been to Germany but she is planning to go there the following year. After her apprenticeship she wants to study mechanical engineering in Bristol.

Frank is a trainee industrial mechanic at VW in Hanover. He is in his third year. He lives at his parents' house in a suburb of Hildesheim. He has already been to England but he has never been to Bristol before. He also wants to study mechanical engineering.

Activity 11, page 14: Answering questions

1. They sent him a letter in which they invite him to come and visit them.
2. The general direction he has to go is north.
3. He has to leave the motorway at junction 12.
4. His friends' home is about three miles away from the motorway.
5. They live in Peregrine Close in Quedgeley, which is a suburb of Gloucester.

Activity 12, page 15: Translation

1. Take the motorway to the North.
2. Drive to the West at junction 14.
3. Turn right at the third traffic light.
4. After two km you will see a roundabout in front of you.
5. Drive into the roundabout and turn towards Cheltenham at the second exit.
6. Follow this road for about half a mile.
7. Then drive straight on at the next traffic light.
8. Turn left at the next traffic light.
9. Turn into Gloucester Road after 200 metres.
10. Look to the left and you will see our house.

Hinweis: The North/the north
"North" wird groß geschrieben, wenn der nördliche Landesteil gemeint ist. Handelt es sich hingegen um die Himmelsrichtung, schreibt man "north" klein.

The North: the northern part of a country
Example: The North will be dry and bright.

The north: in the north or facing the north
Example: The north side of the building does not get much sun.

Activity 13, page 16: Describing the way

a) Drive down Mayville Avenue towards the roundabout. Leave the roundabout at the third exit and drive into Meadowsweet Avenue. At the next crossing there is a church at the left corner. Turn right there and stay on this road until you come to the A 4147. Turn left into Station Road and follow this road until you come to a big roundabout. Leave the roundabout at the opposite side. The road is now called Filton Road. Stay on this road which is later called Avon Ring Road. It leads you directly to the motorway M 32.

b) You end up at Bristol Parkway Station

c) Leave the M 32 at junction 1. Turn right into Avon Ring Road and follow this road. It is later called Filton Road. Drive straight on until you reach a roundabout. Leave this roundabout at the opposite side and carry on until you reach a railway line. Drive under the railway bridge and leave the A 4147 at the next road to the right. Turn right again and after a bend you will see Filton Station to the right.

2 Cars and Tools

Activity 1, page 19: Which car parts do you know?

No.	English	German
1.	headlight	Scheinwerfer
2.	indicator	Blinklicht
3.	bonnet	Motorhaube
4	windscreen wiper	Scheibenwischer
5.	wing mirror	Seitenspiegel
6.	boot	Kofferraum
7.	number plate	Nummernschild
8.	wing	Kotflügel
9.	exhaust pipe	Auspuff(rohr)
10.	bumper	Stoßstange
11.	tyre	Reifen
12.	fuel gauge	Tankanzeige
13	speedometer	Tacho
14.	steering wheel	Steuerrad
15.	gear stick	Schalthebel
16.	handbrake	Handbremse
17.	ignition switch	Zündschloss
18.	accelerator	Gaspedal
19.	brake pedal	Bremspedal
20.	clutch	Kupplung

Activity 2, page 21: Understanding the text

a)
1. False. They are repairing the car at Drake's Garage.
2. False. Keith has got trouble with his battery.
3. True.
4. False. There was no need to replace any fuse.
5. True.
6. False. It is Keith who believes that the alternator does not work.
7. True.

b)
1. – f)
2. – a)
3. – d)
4. – c)
5. – b)
6. – e)

c) Possible answers: spanner, ratchet, Phillips screwdriver, bladed screwdriver, hammer.

Activity 3, page 21: Vocabulary

1. fuse
2. alternator, generator
3. spanner, ratchet
4. battery
5. relay
6. scrap yard
7. twice

Activity 4, page 21: Translation

1. I don't need an open-jawed spanner. Please hand over a ring spanner.
2. I have (already) changed/substituted the battery twice.
3. Where did you buy the battery?
4. A new alternator is quite expensive, isn't it?
5. The new battery is flat again.
6. Overloads can damage the alternator/generator.
7. Two relays don't work.

Activity 5, page 22: Working with tools

a)
1. Ringschlüssel
2. Maulschlüssel
3. Feile
4. Meißel
5. Knarre/Ratsche
6. Nuss
7. Seitenschneider
8. Schraubstock
9. Messschieber
10. Schraubendreher
11. Inbusschlüssel
12. (Flach)Zange
13. Steckschlüssel
14. Lötkolben
15. Multimeter
16. Kreuzschlitzschraubendreher
17. Hobel
18. elektrische Bohrmaschine
19. Kneifzange
20. Säge

b)
1. ring spanner, open-ended spanner
2. ring spanner, open-ended spanner, torque wrench
3. socket wrench
4. multimeter, screwdriver, soldering iron
5. hammer, chisel, side cutter, screwdriver, knife, electric drill
6. hammer, pair of pincers, saw, plane, electric drill

c)
1. tighten/loosen hexagonal nuts
2. tighten/loosen screws
3. solder wires or electronic components
4. cut wires
5. measure voltage/electric current
6. drive nails into wood/walls
7. saw wood/shorten wooden boards
8. pull nails out of wall/wood
9. drill holes into wall

Activity 6, page 23: How to exchange an alternator

Step No.	Action	Tool
1.	Clamp ground from battery	open-ended spanner/ring spanner
2.	Loosen and remove fan belt	open-ended spanner/ring spanner
3.	Remove all plugs and wires from the back of the alternator	screwdriver, pliers
4.	Unscrew alternator	open-ended spanner/ring spanner
5.	Put in new alternator and fasten screws with torque key	open-ended spanner/ring spanner/torque key
6.	Insert all plugs	pliers
7.	Put in fan belt and tighten it	open-ended spanner/ring spanner
8.	Connect ground to negative pole of battery	open ended spanner/ring spanner

Activity 7, page 23: How to give a jump start correctly

1. batteries
2. voltage
3. jump-leads
4. unloaded
5. connect
6. metal part
7. negative pole
8. switch on
9. damage
10. defective
11. remove

Car quiz, page 24

1. **w**indscreen
2. igni**t**ion switch
3. c**l**utch
4. fue**l** gauge
5. indi**c**ator
6. **a**ccelerator
7. bu**m**per
8. **hood**
9. exha**u**st pipe
10. windscreen wipe**r**
11. br**a**ke
12. wi**n**g
13. **t**yre

William Durant

Durant, William C. (1861–1947): The founder of General Motors Corporation. Durant began his career with a horse-drawn carriage company in 1886 and took over Buick in 1904, forming the General Motors (GM) Company in 1908. He lost control in 1910 to Chevrolet but regained ownership in 1915. He was forced out for good in 1920 and founded his own company, Durant Motors, Inc., in 1921.

3 Measuring

Activity 1, page 27: Understanding the text

1. The lady in the weather forecast talked about six inches of rain.
2. Tobias was reminded of his school where he heard about the differences between the metric system used in Germany and the imperial system used in Great Britain.
3. Sarah says that in everyday life everybody talks about inches, feet, pints, and Fahrenheit.
4. Sarah mentions feet (talking about the height of a person), pint (drinking beer in a pub), and degrees Fahrenheit (measuring temperature).
5. Individual answers, e.g.:
   - Square inch = 6,45 cm^2
   - Yard = 91,44 cm
   - Mile = 1,6 km
   - Pound = 453,59 g
   - Gallon (GB) = 4,54 l
   - Gallon (US) = 3,78 l

Activity 2, page 28: Imperial versus metric measures

a) 1. Six inches: 25.4 mm times 6 equals 152.4 mm.
   2. Six feet two: 30.5 cm times 6.2 equals 189.1 cm.
   3. A pint of beer equals 0.57 litre.
   4. 66.2 degrees Fahrenheit equal 19 degrees Celsius:

$$°C = (°F - 32) \times 5/9$$
$$x\ °C = (66.2\ °F - 32) \times 5/9$$
$$x = 19$$

b) 1. 50 m = 166.7 feet
   2. 163 cm = 5.34 feet
   3. 20 °C = 68 °F
   4. –15 °C = 5 °F
   5. 1ℓ = 1.75 pints

c) 1. imperial
   2. pint
   3. Celsius
   4. plus

Activity 3, page 29: Comprehension

a) 1. commonly
   2. manufactured
   3. similarity (oder: if two things are similar)
   4. more precise

b) 1. The system used worldwide is the International System of Units.
2. A common measuring system is necessary because people in business and industry must know whether their manufactured goods achieve certain qualities.
3. Length first was based on a defined unit. Scientists used a special bar as the defined unit for a meter.
4. Now length is defined more precisely. One meter is defined as the distance which light moves in a vacuum in $^1/_{299\ 792\ 458}$ of a second.

Activity 4, page 30: Translation

1. Many centuries different measures were used worldwide never having caused any problems.
2. The metric system is suited best for modern industry and international business (connections).
3. All units of measurement are based on only a few fundamental (basic) units.
4. Velocity, for example, is based on length (distance) and time.

Activity 5, page 30: Instruments for measuring distances

a) 1. geometric triangle
2. folding rule
3. ruler
4. vernier calliper
5. micrometer

b) 1. scale, 2. straight line, 3. length, 4. analogue/digital, 5. angles, 6. metal workers, 7. millimetres, 8. available, 9. distances, 10. technical drawing

Activity 6, page 31: Vernier callipers

a)

No.	German	English
1.	Schiene	main beam/bar
2.	Messschenkel für Innenmessung	inside jaws
3.	Schieber	slider
4,	beweglicher Messschenkel	movable jaw
5.	fester Messchenkel	fixed jaw
6.	Messschenkel für Außenmessung	outside jaws
7.	Feststellschraube	clamp screw
8.	Skala	scale
9.	Tiefenmessgerät	depth bar
10.	Nonien	vernier scale

Activity 7, page 32: What vernier callipers can be used for

1. jaws
2. part
3. external
4. exact
5. fixed
6. movable
7. dimension
8. internal
9. workpiece
10. side

Activity 8, page 32: Vocabulary

a) 1. fixed
   2. screw
   3. scale
   4. opposite
   5. example

b) 1. something manufactured
   2. relating to the inside of something
   3. having the ability to do something
   4. piece of equipment for some special purpose
   5. to leave one position to go to another

Activity 9, page 33: Understanding the text

1. Tom's day was fine, he got an A in his maths test, and physics was quite interesting, too.
2. Tom's mother asks him to help her.
3. Newton was an English scientist.
4. It is the kilogram.
5. The standard measure of one kilogram is a cylinder, made of a special material, with 39 mm in diameter and 39 mm in height.
6. One day Newton was sitting under an apple tree when all of a sudden an apple fell down on his head.

Activity 10, page 34: Newton's law

1. gravitational force
2. Newton
3. kilogram
4. meter
5. second
6. mass
7. kilogram
8. acceleration because of gravity
9. meter per second square (d)

Activity 11, page 35: Talking about Kelvin

Do you know anything about Kelvin?

Yes (sure). Kelvin's name actually was William Thomson. He was born in Ireland in 1824. His father taught him and his brother at home. At the age of ten he began to study at the university of Glasgow. This might sound a little strange for us today but at that time it was not really unusual for intelligent young people. Only five years later he received his first prize. In 1892 he was ennobled and that is why we know him as Lord Kelvin today. He loved his work and was showered with honours. At the age of 75 he decided to leave the field to younger ones. He died in 1907 and is buried in Westminster Abbey in London.

Activity 12, page 35: Instruments for measuring temperature

1. instrument
2. whether
3. weather
4. liquid thermometer
5. capillary tube
6. temperature
7. expands
8. falls
9. measuring
10. bimetallic thermometer
11. expansion
12. scale

Activity 13, page 36: Fundamental laws of science

1. – d)
2. – a)
3. – e)
4. – c)
5. – b)
6. – i)
7. – j)
8. – f)
9. – h)
10. – g)

Activity 14, page 37: Understanding the text

1. Kathy and David are apprentices.
2. They are in the workshop at the moment.
3. David is showing Kathy how to work with a multimeter.
4. David mentions a display, a range selector, and two leads with a probe tip each.
5. a) ampere (amp), symbol A
   b) volt, symbol V
6. Current must flow through the consumer.
7. If you want to measure voltage, you have to connect the multimeter in parallel.

Activity 15, page 37: Measuring electric current

1. measuring
2. ammeter
3. circle
4. order
5. electric current
6. in series

Activity 16, page 37: Measuring voltage

1. symbol
2. circuit diagram
3. centre
4. measure
5. in parallel

4 Health and Safety at Work

Activity 1, page 41: Understanding the text

a) 1. Ann and Mike know each other from vocational school. They are in the same class.
2. Mike was not at school today.
3. The accident happened to Mike yesterday when he has almost finished work.
4. Mike wanted to sharpen his knife. He was in a hurry, so he decided not to wear protective goggles.
5. The doctor removed a splinter from Mike's eye.
6. Mike's eye feels like there is still some sand inside.
7. Ann and Mike are laughing about Mike's joke. He said from now on he would always wear protective goggles even when he was sharpening a pencil.
8. Ann wants to visit Mike later.

b) Possible answer:
One day my friend Peter was working in the workshop on a running engine of a bus. The place he was standing at was dirty with spilled oil from the previous job which he had not cleaned up. Peter slipped and lost balance. He tried to hold onto something (to keep his balance) but unfortunately his hand got caught in the running engine and cut off a fingertip. All in all he was lucky not to lose his whole hand.

Activity 2, page 42: Working with words

a) 1. falling down
2. lung disease
3. falls
4. grinding
5. hearing damage

b) 1. Safety at work protects everybody.
2. Safety equipment is necessary for the safety of everybody.
3. A first aid kit is important to have at home too.
4. Some toxic gases are odourless.
5. Loud noises can impair/damage your hearing.
6. A clean workplace is an important defence against accidents.
7. Accident prevention is an issue for everybody.

Activity 3, page 42: Talking about safety

a) Possible answers:
1. The nearest first aid box is at the caretaker's office. (Give an accurate description)
2. I leave this room, turn to the left and go down the stairs to the ground floor. The caretaker's office is at the end of the corridor. It is the last door on the right-hand side. On the right-hand side of the door is a button which calls the caretaker. (Give accurate description)
3. Wearing personal protective equipment is your first line of defence against accidents.

4. Somebody could drink the toxic liquid accidentally, thinking it might be something to drink. Serious injuries could be caused.
5. Safety is more than following rules. To be truly safe, make safe work habits second nature. Take responsibility for noticing, reporting, and correcting hazards. Take care of everybody.

b) Possible answers:
Hairnet; used on turning devices. Long hair is easily tangled in drive shafts or drills.
Guard; used on machines and devices with dangerous points. It prevents the operator or other persons coming into contact with dangerous points.
Lifting crane; for lifting and manual handling of heavy loads. It prevent injuries to the back caused by manual handling of heavy loads.
Ladder; used when working in higher positions. It guarantees a suitable and safer standing platform.
Know how; required for anything we do. It prevents carelessness and makes you aware of typical dangers.

Activity 4, page 44: Questions

1. Warning sings are yellow coloured with a black periphery. They are triangular. Specific hazards can be indicated by black symbols.
2. Prohibition sings and warning sings differ in colour and form. Warning signs require a specific action whilst prohibition signs stipulate behaviour.
3. First aid signs identify locations of first aid facilities such like stretcher and first aid kits. Emergency signs identify a secure escape in case of fire or other hazard situations.
4. Warning signs are located in areas where specific hazards are unpredictable. They require special and specific attention.
5. In hazardous areas the warning signs have black symbols or they have additional information.

Activity 5, page 45: Understanding the text

1. ... wounds, what to do in case of unconsciousness, how to place somebody in the recovery position and much more.
2. ... needed to ensure that first aid is available at all times.
3. ... expire after some time.
4. ... observing signs and safety regulations.
5. ... safety.
6. ... from danger.
7. ... for help.

Activity 6, page 46: Working with words

1. seconds
2. discharged
3. instructions
4. familiarised
5. hands-on
6. walk
7. refill

Activity 7, page 47: How to use a fire extinguisher

1. g)
2. c)
3. a)
4. h)
5. d)
6. i)
7. j)
8. e)
9. b)
10. f)

Activity 8, page 47: Questions

1. I have to be familiarised with the parts of the fire extinguisher.
2. When the fire extinguisher is used on electrical equipment the minimum distance is one metre.
3. I fight burning liquid from the top with a wide stream of powder.
4. The fire extinguisher contains extinguishing powder for ten seconds.
5. I have to make sure not to return the cylinder to its place. The used cylinder has to be replaced or to be refilled immediately.

Activity 9, page 48: Fill a form

a) Individual answer:

<table>
<tr><td colspan="2"></td><td colspan="2">ACCIDENT/INCIDENT
REPORT</td><td>Safety Office
494-2495</td></tr>
<tr><td rowspan="3">PERSONAL</td><td>Surname: Mike</td><td colspan="2">First name: Frampton</td><td>Date: 2008-11-10</td></tr>
<tr><td colspan="4">Home Address: Barker Street, Bristol, DN5 7LY</td></tr>
<tr><td colspan="2">Department: Metal</td><td colspan="2">Phone: 987 654 321</td></tr>
<tr><td rowspan="3">INCIDENT</td><td colspan="2">Date, Time and Location of Incident:
2008-11-10, 4:55 pm, workshop</td><td colspan="2">Name and Phone of Witnesses:
None</td></tr>
<tr><td colspan="4">Describe the incident in detail: While sharpening a tool a splinter hit into the eye.</td></tr>
<tr><td colspan="2">When and to whom was the incident reported? Workshop manager</td><td colspan="2">Did the incident result in an early departure from work? ☐ Yes ☒ No</td></tr>
<tr><td rowspan="3">INJURY</td><td colspan="4">Describe injuries:
Foreign-body (splinter) entered the eye. It was not removable by first aid treatment.</td></tr>
<tr><td colspan="4">Briefly describe medical treatment, if needed: Eye covered with an eye-patch</td></tr>
<tr><td colspan="2">Will the injury result in time away from work beyond the day of the incident? ☐ Yes ☒ No</td><td colspan="2">Will further treatment be necessary?
☒ Yes ☐ No</td></tr>
<tr><td colspan="2">Date: 2008-11-10</td><td colspan="3">Person involved in incident: None</td></tr>
</table>

b) When Mike was almost finished with work he wanted to sharpen his knife on a bench grinder. He was in a hurry so he didn't want to waste time looking for some protective goggles. As soon as the knife touched the grinding disc a splinter hit his eye.
Mike was not able to continue sharpening his knife; he had to see the doctor immediately.
The doctor removed the splinter from Mike's eye.
All this happened because Mike did not wear protective goggles.

Activity 10, page 48: Comprehension

1. False. Watch the area for a few minutes in case it re-ignites.
2. True.
3. True.
4. True
5. False. Always read the instruction that comes with the fire extinguisher beforehand and get familiarised with its parts.
6. True.

5 Computer Hardware

Activity 1, page 51: Parts of a computer system

a)

No.	Component	No.	Component
1	computer (desktop)	6	(cordless/wireless) mouse
2	monitor	7	(cordless/wireless) keyboard
3	scanner	8	external HDD
4	printer	9	USB memory stick
5	joy stick	10	router

b) No.4: Drucker; No.6: (schnurlose) Maus; No.7: (schnurlose) Tastatur; No.8: externe Festplatte

c) Technical data (examples)

a) **computer**
processor: AMD Athlon 64 Dual Core with 2.6 GHz; RAM: 2048 MB DDR 2; HDD: SATA 80 GB etc.

b) **monitor**
19" TFT monitor; contrast ratio: 1000:1; resolution: 1280 × 1024; response time: 8 ms

c) **printer**
print technology: thermal inkjet; print speed: up to 2.5 ppm (normal quality black and color); resolution: 1200 × 600 dpi; number of cartridges: 4; connectivity: USB

d) **USB memory stick**
USB stick 4 GB with software 'carry it easy'; read: 18.5 MB/s; write: 2.5 MB/s

Activity 2, page 51: Abbreviations

No.	Abbreviation	Complete word
1	RAM	Random Access Memory (Speicher mit beliebigem Zugriff)
2	CD-ROM	Compact Disk – Read Only Memory (Nur-Lese-Speicher)
3	Mbps	Megabits per second (Einheit für Datenübertragungsrate)
4	CPU	Central Processing Unit (Zentraleinheit, andere Bezeichnung für 'Prozessor')
5	GB	Gigabyte
6	DVD	Digital Versatile Disk (Datenträger mit sehr hoher Aufzeichnungsdichte; versatile = vielseitig)
7	BIOS	Basic Input Output System (Basissoftware zum Booten des PC)
8	PC	Personal Computer

No.	Abbreviation	Complete word
9	SATA	Serial Advanced Technology Attachment (spezieller Datenbus für den Datentransfer zwischen Prozessor und Festplatte)
10	ISDN	Integrated Services Digital Network (dienstintegriertes digitales Netzwerk)
11	MPEG	Moving Picture Expert Group (Standard, der Verfahren zur Audio- und Videodatenkompression beschreibt)
12	GHz	Gigahertz
13	USB	Universal Serial Bus (serielles Bussystem zur Verbindung von Peripheriegeräten mit dem Computer)
14	W-LAN	Wireless Local Area Network (drahtloses lokales Netzwerk)

Activity 3, page 51: Working with words

1. printer
2. hard disk
3. processor
4. joystick
5. monitor
6. scanner
7. USB memory stick
8. hub
9. sound card
10. mouse

Activity 4, page 53: Comprehension

1. CPU, memory, bus system, controllers, expansion slots
2. It performs all logic operation of the computer.
3. It consists of a piece of silicon with millions of transistors on it.
4. The BIOS first checks if the most important components work properly and then searches and loads the Operating System.
5. RAM is a temporary memory which means that the stored data disappears when the power supply is switched off whereas ROM keeps its data in this case. In opposite to RAM you can't write data to ROM, only read them.
6. It is a kind of highway on which data travel. Buses are the connection between the CPU and the peripherals.
7. Bus width is a measure for the amount of data (number of bits) that is transferred on a data bus at the same time.
8. It is either a cable made of a certain number of parallel wires or a certain number of parallel conductor lines on a printed circuit board.
9. It is measured in Hertz (MHz, GHz).
10. Bi-directional: data travel in both directions
    Uni-directional: data travel only in one direction (from CPU to memory or other components)

Activity 5, page 53: Working with words

1. circuit board
2. data
3. memory
4. BIOS

Activity 6, page 53: Modems

1. demodulator
2. receive
3. convert
4. digital data
5. transmitted
6. networks
7. services
8. speeds
9. communicate
10. highest

Activity 7, page 55: Comprehension

1. Alan is an experienced computer user./Alan has been an experienced computer user for many years.
2. Bert has bought a used computer.
3. Bert has got trouble with his sound/with his sound card.
4. Alan comes to Bert's place.
5. Alan suggests to check whether the driver for the sound card has been installed correctly.
6. Bert has already checked the installation of the driver.
7. They only need a Phillips screwdriver.
8. They have to install a new driver.

Activity 8, page 56: Changing a sound card

First, they have to check if the computer meets the system requirements. Then they must turn off the computer and unplug all peripherals. After having opened the casing, they should loosen the screws of the old sound card and remove it from its slot. After that they can insert the new sound card and fasten it with the bracket and the screws. However, before taking the new sound card out of its bag they must make sure that they have taken precautions against static electricity. Finally, they can close the casing and connect all cables.

Activity 9, page 56: Translation

1. Alan has got a lot of experience with computers.
2. Bert bought the used computer four weeks ago.
3. Bert has got trouble with the sound of his computer.
4. The fault only occurs when he opens a file on a DVD.
5. First we have to check if the driver of the sound card has been installed correctly.

6. Alan suggests to change the sound card.
7. We only need a Phillips screwdriver to open the casing.
8. Where do I find the driver for the new sound card?
9. Have you reinserted all plugs and cables?
10. The system has discovered the new hardware.

Activity 10, page 56: Mounting a second HDD

1. Turn your computer off and unplug it from the mains.
2. Unplug all peripheral devices attached to the computer.
3. Remove the cover from your computer.
4. Remove the cover plate from the drive slot.
5. Make sure that you have set the jumpers at the new HDD correctly. The second HDD must be connected as slave.
6. Connect the 40-pin IDE cable to the back of the new drive.
7. Make sure that the red edge of the IDE cable is connected to Pin 1 on the new hard disk drive.
8. Slide the new drive into the drive slot and secure the drive in place with screws.
9. Push the power supply cable connector firmly into the power in connector.
10. Boot the computer and if necessary install the new driver.

6 Software

Activity 1, page 60: Vocabulary

1. – g)
2. – d)
3. – f)
4. – a)
5. – b)
6. – c)
7. – e)

Activity 2, page 60: Definitions

1. overview
2. preparation
3. e-mail
4. leaflet
5. Internet

Activity 3, page 60: Questions

1. Which operating system is installed on your computer?
2. Which application software do you have installed and what do you do with it?
3. Which software do you have installed on your PC but never used it?
4. How much time do you spend at your computer professionally?
5. What do you use the Internet for?

Activity 4, page 60: Making predictions

Possible answers:
I am sure that in a couple of years every student has got his own laptop and does his tests online.
I think that computers will be good for elder people. They can do their shopping online and have everything brought to their home.
Women might prefer to work at home as long as their children are too young to go to a kindergarden. They have an online connection to their company and can choose their working hours themselves.

Activity 5, page 62: Understanding the text

1. True.
2. False. She has just bought a new computer, her first one.
3. False. The company has its own intranet.
4. True.
5. False. Software has to be updated regularly.
6. False. Sometimes the company has to buy a completely new software after a short period of time.
7. False. Every user has his own password.
8. False. Every employee has access according to his needs and tasks.
9. False. They only need training when the company buys new software.
10. False. The system is not safe against attacks from outside.

Activity 6, page 62: Working with words

1. links
2. staff member
3. renewed
4. admission
5. stable
6. frequently
7. took part in
8. trainee
9. provides

Activity 7, page 62: Working with words

1. to attend
2. unusual
3. to refuse
4. virus
5. customer
6. explain
7. password
8. develop

Activity 8 page 64: Understanding the text

1. Advantages are: You can store and save files, you can create three-dimensional objects, you can change parts of a drawing any time, CAD is vector oriented, you can program a CNC machine.
2. At the top of the screen you find the menu bar, at the bottom you have command lines, on the left side of the screen you can place a toolkit.
3. Layers are like transparent sheets which are put on top of each other. All together they show the finished drawing.
4. Layers can be turned on and off, they can be used separately, and each layer can be assigned to a special line type, colour or thickness.
5. Editing means to change or alter drawings quickly, e.g. by trimming, which enables the user to take away parts of lines in drawings, by mirroring, which makes an object move around an axis, or by copying, which creates as many similar object as the user wishes.
6. CAD programs are vector oriented. If you have e.g. 600 mm on screen, you also have got 600 mm on paper, what makes it possible to program a CNC machine with data from the CAD drawing.
7. Companies can use CAD drawings to program a CNC machine because CAD is vector oriented.

Activity 9 page 64: Working with words

1. drawing commands
2. command line
3. menu bar
4. different layers
5. program
6. data

Activity 10 page 64: Word search

a)

										I	C	O	N				
P	T									I	O					T	L
	R			L			F		R		M					E	A
	I	O			A		I	C			M					E	C
	M		G			Y	L				A					H	I
	M			R		E	E				N	E	E	R	C	S	R
	I				A		S	R			D						E
	N					M			C								M
	G								A								U
									D	I	M	E	N	S	I	O	N

CAD, circle, command, dimension, files, icon, layer, numerical, program, screen, sheet, trimming

b) Possible answers:
1. CAD stands for computer aided design.
2. Please draw a circle with a diameter of 10 cm.
3. The command 'Mirroring' makes the object move around an axis.
4. Layers in a drawing are like transparent sheets.
5. Trimming enables you to take away parts of lines.

Activity 11 page 65: Practice

a) Dargestellt ist jeweils eine mögliche Lösung. Selbstverständlich sind auch andere Lösungen möglich.

b) Individual answers.

1. Aufgabe:

2. Aufgabe:

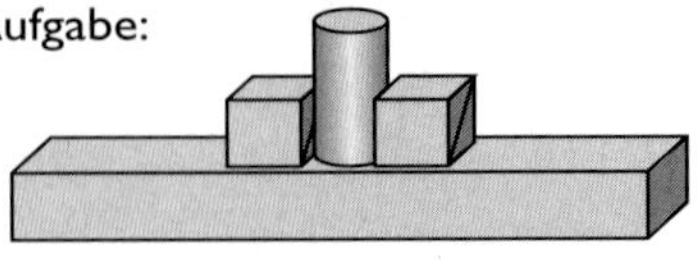

7 Power Tools and Machines

Activity 1, page 68: Tools and their applications

No.	Name	Explanation
1.	jig saw	A jig saw is used for cutting shapes into thin pieces of wood or metal.
2.	electric drill	You can drill holes into different materials like wood or metal with an electric drill.
3.	planer	A planer is used to make the surface of a wooden workpiece smooth.
4.	cordless drill and screwdriver	This tool is used for drilling holes and screwing screws into wood.
5.	circular saw	This type of saw is used for cutting wood.
6.	triangular base-plate sander	This tool can be used for sanding wood, plastic, metal and paintwork
7.	belt sander	This tool can be used for sanding the surfaces of wooden workpieces very rapidly.

Activity 2, page 69: Matching technical terms

No.	English	German
1.	power cord	Netzkabel
2.	chuck key	Futterschlüssel
3.	trigger	Schalter
4.	handle	Griff
5.	chuck	Bohrkopf, Futter
6.	drill bit	Bohrwerkzeug, Bohrer

Activity 3, page 69: Understanding the text

1. Drilling holes into different materials is one of the most frequent tasks at home or in the workshop. Apart from that an electric drill can be adapted for different jobs by adding various equipment.
2. The cutting speed of a drill bit increases with its diameter. To keep the cutting speed constant you have to lower the number of revolutions.
3. Electronically controlled electric drills allow to adjust the revolutions to the cutting speed needed.
4. The chuck is used to clamp the drill bit.
5. If you do not remove the chuck key before starting the drill, the key will loosen and may injure you or your work mates.
6. An electric drill is started by pressing the trigger and stopped by releasing the trigger.

Activity 4, page 70: Describing an action

First, remove the power cord from the power supply. Then open the chuck with the chuck key and remove the drill bit. Next, choose the drill bit and insert it into the open mouth of the chuck. Use the chuck key again to close the chuck and clamp the drill bit. Do not forget to remove the chuck key before you connect the power cord with the power supply and start the electric drill.

Activity 5, page 71: Matching exercise

1. – e)
2. – f)
3. – d)
4. – a)
5. – g)
6. – b)
7. – c)

Activity 6, page 71: Describing an action

1. power supply
2. saw clamp screw
3. tool
4. remove
5. saw blade
6. teeth
6. a) upwards
7. saw
8. screw
9. saw blade
10. flange

First draw a guideline across the board. Then place the front of the saw base on the work piece so that the guide line and the front plate are in one line. Make sure that the saw blade does not touch the work piece before you press the trigger to start the saw. After starting the saw let the blade revolve at full speed. After that push the saw forward slowly so that the blade can start cutting.
If the cutting is finished release the trigger and wait until the rotation of the blade has come to a standstill. In the end put the saw back onto the work bench.

Activity 8, page 73: Understanding safety regulations

1. Safety regulations are important because you cannot see electricity and an electric shock is very dangerous. It can even kill you. In addition, electric tools can be very powerful. They may cause serious injuries if you do not use them properly.
2. You should either ask someone who is in charge to show you how to operate the machine or read the operating instruction in the manual carefully.
3. All power tools should be in a proper state of repair and always clean before you use them.
4. Loose sleeves can be caught by the rotating parts of a power tool and you can seriously be injured.
5. The rotating tool has a lot of power and can injure you or your workmates.
6. Sharp objects can penetrate the power cord and cause a short circuit.
7. Electric power tools cause sparks and they can ignite explosives or inflammable gases.

Activity 9, page 73: Safety signs

1. Wear googles
2. Wear a hard hat
3. Wear breathing mask
4. Wear eye protection
5. Use bridge
6. Fire and open light are not allowed
7. Keep away
8. Mobile phones not allowed
9. Don not touch, high voltage
10. Fork lifts not allowed
11. Warning: laser radiation
12. Warning: dangerous voltage
13. Warning: gas cylinders
14. Warning: explosives
15. Warning: industrial trucks
16. Direction for rescue
17. First aid
18. Emergency exit
19. Emergency exit to the left

Activity 10, page 74: Matching the parts of a lathe

Letter	English	German
a)	chuck	Spannfutter
b)	position display	Positionsanzeige
c)	tailstock	Reitstock
d)	carriage feed shaft	Zugspindel
e)	leadscrew	Leitspindel
f)	emergency switch	Notausschalter
g)	cross slide	Querschlitten
h)	feedgear levers	Vorschubgetriebehebel
i)	safety cover	Schutzhaube
j)	head stock	Spindelstock
k)	swarf tray	Spänewanne
l)	engine frame	Maschinenbett
m)	revolution levers	Schalthebel für Drehzahlen

Activity 11, page 75: Understanding the text

1. Shape cutting chipping is performed by a cutting tool which gives the work piece its shape by cutting off chips. Chipless shaping is a forming process in which the work piece receives its shape by bending, for example, without cutting off chips.
2. Turning and milling are the most important processing methods of shaping metal.
3. In the turning process all kinds of workpieces which are symmetrical with respect to their rotation axis can be produced, for example, cylindrical or cone-shaped workpieces.
4. In the turning process the workpiece performs the cutting movement, whereas the tool performs the feed movement and the depth setting.
5. Modern milling machines are able to produce a large variety of shapes. Even three-dimensional curves can be produced, but mainly flat surfaces are milled.
6. The milling head can be pivoted between the vertical position and the horizontal position, i.e. between 0° and 90° at any angle.
7. In the milling process the tool performs the cutting movement and the work piece carries out the feed movement and depth setting.
8. The milling cutter is usually clamped in the milling spindle.
9. The main differences are the tools and the parts of the machine that perform the different movements of the tools and work pieces.
10. Both machines are powered by an electric motor. They both shape the work piece with tools that have geometrically defined cutting edges. The power of the motor is transmitted to the spindle via a gear box.

Activity 12, page 77: Understanding the dialogue

1. Mr Smith tells the two boys that one of the old milling machines does not work properly.
2. John thinks the best way to start is by reading the instruction manual.
3. They can find the instruction manual on the shelf in Mr Smith's office.
4. It is the milling machine in the middle at the side of the training workshop.
5. He does not like them because they fail almost every week.
6. They press the on/off switch.
7. The spindle starts turning. So it cannot be an electrical problem.
8. a) By hand, with the help of a cranked handle and b) by means of the automatic feed.

Activity 13, page 77: Translation

1. The instruction manual for the milling machine is lying on the shelf in Mr Smith's office.
2. There are three old milling machines in the training workshop.
3. John has often worked with the milling machine and he knows how to operate it.
4. The main switch has to be put into position I and then the button must be pressed.
5. This lever must completely be pushed back clockwise.
6. It is not an electrical problem because the spindle starts turning.

7. It says in the manual that there are two different ways of longitudinal adjustment.
8. There is something wrong with the automatic feed.
9. The adjustable stops are in the right position.
10. The trainees find out that there is a fault in the automatic feed system.

Activity 14, page 77: Making questions

1. Where does the manual for the milling machine lie?
2. How many milling machines are there in the workshop?
3. What does John know?
4. How do you start the machine?
5. Why does John hate that machine?
6. What is wrong with the automatic feed.
7. Who will give us the new belt?

Activity 15, page 78: Translation

Auswechseln des Riemens:
Schalten Sie den Motor aus und heben Sie die Abdeckung an und öffnen Sie die Tür. Drehen Sie den Handgriff nach oben, um die Riemen zu entspannen. Ersetzen Sie die Riemen. Drehen Sie den Handgriff nach unten, überprüfen Sie die Riemenspannung und schließen Sie die Abdeckung und die Tür bevor Sie die Maschine wieder einschalten.

Achtung:
Der Motor und der Motorträger sollten durch den Spanner und nicht durch den Riemen gehalten werden. Der Handgriff sollte immer in der vertikalen Position sein. Justieren Sie die Spannung des Riemens für das Vorschubgetriebe, indem Sie das Getriebe vertikal verschieben. Dazu sollten die 4 Haltebolzen des Getriebes leicht gelockert werden.

8 Environment

Activity 1, page 81: Getting into the unit

1. Sources of air pollution are car engines, factories, firestorms, volcanoes, and airplanes. Volcanoes and sometimes firestorms are natural sources. Man-made sources are car engines, airplanes, factories, and sometimes firestorms if somebody sets a forest on fire intentionally.

2. Examples for effects of emission:
   - on human beings are: cancer, allergies, influences of poisonous heavy metals on liver, kidneys, and bones.
   - on plants are: trees are dying
   - on buildings are: corrosion (metal), destruction of facades.

Activity 2, page 82: Partner work

1. Regina's questions are:
   - When the sun shines, do you use your bicycle instead of your car?
   - Do you drive in car pools?
   - Do you use rechargeable batteries?
   - Do you leave your appliances on stand-by?

2. Possible questions are:
   - Do you sort waste?
   - Do you buy beverages in bottles?
   - How often do you wash your car?
   - Do you water your lawn in summer?
   - If you had to buy a new car, would you buy one consuming less petrol? Would you buy it, even if it was more expensive?

3. Individual answers.

Activity 3, page 83: Understanding the text

1. Air pollution is a global problem because there are no boundaries in the atmosphere. Analytic measurements in regions without any industry, e.g. the Antarctic, have proved that the air is polluted there, too.
2. Chlorofluorocarbons are responsible for the hole in the ozone layer.
3. The hole in the ozone layer is mainly responsible for skin cancer.
4. Exhaust fumes cause smog and acid rain.
5. Almost every car is equipped with a catalytic converter. Cars use less petrol.
6. If the ozone concentration is too high, drivers of older vehicles have to leave their cars at home and students are not allowed to do any sports outside.
7. Mainly responsible are the carbon dioxide emissions, which derive from the burning of e.g. mineral oil.
8. The results of the greenhouse effect and the global warming are the rise of water levels and heavy storms with large rainfalls.

Activity 4, page 84: Working with words

a) 1. catalytic converter
2. concentration
3. reduced
4. analytic measurements
5. traffic lights

b)

		R								E							
			E		E	L	I	H	W	N	A	E	M				T
	L	L	N	N						E							N
	O		G		W	I	N	T	E	R	T	I	M	E			E
H	R		I			O				G		R	E	V	I	R	D
	T		N							Y					R		U
	E		E	V	E	R	Y	B	O	D	Y				A		T
	P					C	O	N	S	E	Q	U	E	N	C	E	S

car, consequences, driver, energy, engine, everybody, hole, meanwhile, owner, petrol, student, wintertime

Possible answers:
1. Meanwhile every student, who is a car owner, tries to save petrol.
2. Everybody knows of the consequences if he lets his car engine run in the wintertime.

Activity 5, page 84: Consequences of air pollution

1. – d)
2. – c)
3. – c)
4. – d)
5. – b)
6. – b)
7. – a)
8. – a)

Activity 6, page 85: Environmental impacts on buildings

a) 1. acid
2. limestone
3. necessary
4. original
5. facade
6. figure
7. scaffolding
8. stone-masons
9. damages
10. attempt
11. carvings

b) Possible answers:
1. Cars ought to be forbidden in inner cities.
2. More cars using little petrol should be produced.
3. A speed limit on highways must be obligatory.

Activity 7, page 86: Statements

1. False. Although about 80% of the earth's surface is covered with water, most of it is salt water and cannot be used for nutrition.
2. True.
3. False. The water produced by these plants is very expensive.
4. False. We consume 4 litres a day for drinking and cooking.
5. False. Most of the earth's surface is covered with salt water.

Activity 8, page 86: From ground water to drinking water

1. is filtrated
2. are eaten
3. is pumped
4. is extracted
5. would be destroyed
6. has to be passed
7. is filtrated
8. can be filled

Activity 9, page 86: Comprehension

a) Examples are:
- Take a shower instead of a bath.
- Forbid people to water their lawn in summer.
- Do not wash your car too often.
- Collect rain water to water your plants.
- Build a well in your garden and use the collected water for your laundry, washing your car, and flushing the toilet.

b) Individual answers.

Activity 10, page 88: Questions

a) 1. Not everybody is interested in the subject. Some people do not want to be interviewed. However, most persons she asked were helpful and willing to exchange ideas.
2. A new party in the political scene has come up.
3. People are now aware that they have to protect nature not only for the living but even more for the coming generations.
4. Schools try to save energy, reduce and sort waste.
5. Koryn thinks that environmental protection is important.
6. Americans love plain water for drinking. A lot of Germans buy their water in bottles.
7. Regina tries to save water. She bought a car that consumes little fuel.

b) 1. Who loves plain water?
2. What do the best schools get?
3. Where have environmental problems been discussed for years?
4. What can be seen on TV?
5. What is the job like?
6. How can the environment be protected?
7. For how long have environmental problems been discussed?

Activity 11, page 88: A catalytic converter

1. catalytic converter
2. reduce
3. processes
4. lack
5. cancer
6. modern
7. low
8. principle
9. catalyst
10. value

Activity 12, page 89: Discussion

a) A catalytic converter has a honeycomb-like structure. The exhaust fumes are conducted through very thin channels, which enlarge the active area for conversion. The ceramic honeycombs are covered with platinum. A catalytic converter changes toxic substances into more harmless ones: Nitrogen oxides become nitrogen, carbon monoxide becomes carbon dioxide, and hydrocarbons become carbon dioxide and water.

Beachten Sie: Dies ist eine sehr vereinfachte Darstellung, die speziell für Auszubildende zum Kraftfahrzeugmechatroniker oder andere interessierte Schüler detailgetreuer ausgearbeitet werden kann.

b) Individual answers.
The advantages of a catalytic converter are listed. They can be used as basis for discussion.

c) Disadvantages are:
- A catalytic converter works effectively only after the operating temperature has been reached.
- Emission of toxic substances is also possible at low temperatures.
- Essential is the lamda probe (A = 1) which must control the mixture of air and fuel.
- After some time the catalytic converter has to be exchanged.

Activity 13, page 89: Working with words

a)
1. rust
2. incineration plant
3. tax (es)
4. technician
5. poisonous

b) Possible answers:
1. something with leaves that grows in the earth (plant, tree)
2. something that is given to somebody who has won a competition (prize)
3. material that is useless or unwanted (waste)

9 Energy

Activity 1, page 93: Warm up

a)

No.	Machine/appliance	Kind of energy
1.	aeroplane	kerosene
2.	car	petrol
3.	vacuum cleaner	electricity
4.	hair-dryer	electricity
5.	(fire-view) stove	wood
6.	iron	electricity
7.	cassette recorder	electricity
8.	robots	electricity
9.	truck	diesel

b)

Applience	Energy consumption
washing machine	2–2.5 kW
electric kitchen stove	8–10 kW
TV Set	50–200 kW
freezer	0.8 kW per 24h
camcorder	3–4 W
blender	300–400 W
refrigerator	1 kWh per 24h

Applience	Energy consumption
central heating	15 kW
printer	25 W when printing
light bulb	60/100 W etc.
mobile phone	D-Netz: 0.8–8 W
toaster	800–1000 W
dish washer	2.5 kW

Activity 2, page 95: Understanding the text

1. We need energy to power our vehicles, warm our homes, cook our food, and when we want to be entertained (TV, radio).
2. Energy is defined as the ability to do work.
3. A power plant is a place/factory where electricity is generated.
4. Every thermal power plant converts energy into heat energy which is used to change water into steam.
5. Steam is produced in big boilers and conducted to (a) turbine(s). under high pressure. When the steam hits the blades of the turbine, it starts turning.
6. A generator consists of a stationary ring which is wrapped with a long wire (also called the stator) and a magnet which turns inside the stator (called the rotor).
7. Power plants need huge amounts of cooling water, therefore they are built near rivers and lakes.

8. Cooling towers are needed to cool down the cooling water before it flows back into the river or lake.
9. The splitting up of atoms is called nuclear fission.
10. A nuclear power plant produces steam like a coal power station to spin the turbine.

Activity 3, page 96: Comprehension

1. The common voltage at the sockets in our homes is 230 V.
2. Transformers boost up the voltages for the transport to the consumer.
3. Electricity is transported in cables made of copper or aluminium.
4. If the diameter of the cables increases the resistance will decrease.
5. Using high voltages can keep the flow of electric current low.
6. The size of the high-voltage poles depends on the voltage in the cables.
7. Most transmission lines within cities are underground lines.
8. At our homes the electricity is measured by an energy meter

Activity 4, page 96: Working with words

1. electric current
2. power plant
3. cable
4. turbine
5. cooling tower
6. uranium
7. generator
8. magnet
9. pole
10. transformer
11. nuclear fission
12. energy meter

Activity 5, page 96: Translation

1. Energy can neither be created nor used up/destroyed.
2. Electricity is generated in power plants.
3. Thermal power plants have big boilers to produce steam.
4. The steam is conducted to the turbines under high pressure.
5. Thermal power plants need a lot of water to cool down the steam.
6. For that reason thermal power plants are built near rivers or lakes.
7. In nuclear power plants uranium atoms are split up to produce heat.
8. If a conductor/wire moves across a magnetic field, an electric voltage is generated in it.
9. The transmission of energy requires high voltages.
10. Electric energy is transmitted in cables that are fixed at high voltage poles.

Activity 6, page 97: Nuclear fission

1. atom
2. protons
3. electrons
4. split
5. energy
6. generate
7. explosion
8. reactor
9. uranium atoms
10. particles
11. chain reaction
12. heat energy
13. boil
14. turbine

Activity 7, page 97: Word Search

v															
o						p						g			
l			m		n	u	c	l	e	a	r	e			
t	t	r	a	n	s	m	i	s	s	i	o	n			
a	u		g			p			h			e			
g	r		n						a			r			
e	b		e	n	e	r	g	y	f		c	a	b	l	e
	i		t						t		s	t	e	a	m
	n											o			
	e								c	u	r	r	e	n	t

voltage, turbine, magnet, pump, shaft, generator, nuclear, transmission, energy, cable, steam, current

Activity 8, page 98: Talking about alternative energy sources

a) 1. solar energy (photovoltaic generator)
   2. wind energy
   3. solar energy (solar thermal systems)
   4. geothermal energy (Old Faithful, Yellowstone National Park, USA)
   5. hydro energy/water power (the photograph shows the Hoover Dam in Arizona, USA)
   6. biomass energy (dung)

Das Bild 3 zeigt ein Solarfarm-Kraftwerk.
Solarfarmen „ernten“ Sonnenenergie auf großen Flächen mit Rinnenkollektoren. Diese bestehen aus lang gestreckten Spiegelsegmenten in parabolischer Form, die das eingefangene Sonnenlicht in ihrem Brennpunkt konzentrieren, der von Röhren durchzogen ist. Die Neigung der Kollektoren lässt sich nach dem Stand der Sonne ausrichten. Ein Wärmeträger, z.B. ein spezielles Öl, durchfließt die Röhren und wird auf rund 400 °C erhitzt. In einem Wärmetauscher gibt das Öl seine Wärmeenergie ab und Dampf zum Antrieb einer Turbine wird erzeugt. Statt Öl in den Kollektoren zu erhitzen, ist es alternativ möglich und auch billiger, Wasser zu verdampfen. In den 1980er-Jahren wurden neun Rinnenkollektor-Kraftwerke in der Mojave-Wüste (USA) mit insgesamt 354 MW gebaut.

b) Individual answers, e.g.:
- river power plant
- pumping plant and reservoir
- dam
- wind turbines
- photovoltaic systems to generate electricity
- solar thermal systems to produce heat, e.g. domestic hot water systems
- biomass (wide range of applications, e.g. landfill gas)

c) Individual answers, e.g.:
- Tidal energy: Tidal range at German coasts not efficient.
- Geothermal energy: The production of electric energy through geothermal heat is mainly used in volcanic regions.

Activity 9, page 100: Comprehension

1. Rotor, shaft, rotating parts inside the transmission box, and rotating parts of the generator (also called rotor).
2. The transmission box increases the speed of rotation so that the generator turns fast enough to generate electricity.
3. The height of the tower depends on the lengths of the rotor blades.
4. The yaw system turns the rotor blades (or complete nacelle) into the best direction so that the wind hits the blades either directly or from behind.
5. A possible construction site must be checked carefully to find out whether the average wind speed at that place is high enough to produce electricity economically.
6. Advantages are:
   - The wind blows stronger at the sea.
   - This kind of wind park does not disturb scenic landscape (not in text).

   Disadvantages are:
   - Wind turbines must be able to withstand stronger storms.
   - It is more difficult to fix a tower in the sea bed than putting it up on land.
7. Students have to convert metres per second into miles per hour. Five metres per second equals 29 mph which according to the diagram leads to a 100% power output.
8. The wind speed is about 25 mph which equals 4.3 metres per second.

Activity 10, page 101: The Alternative Energy Quiz

1. – b)	7. – b)	13. – d)
2. – c)	8. – c)	14. – d)
3. – c)	9. – b)	15. – c)
4. – c)	10. – b)	16. – c)
5. – d)	11. – d)	
6. – b)	12. – c)	

Activity 11, page 103: Comprehension

1. Which gas is mainly responsible for heating up the earth's atmosphere?
2. Why is it so difficult to persuade people to use public transportation?
3. What happens if hydrogen is burnt in an internal combustion engine?
4. How does a fuel cell work?
5. Where have fuel cells been used for many years?
6. How can hydrogen be stored in cars?
7. Why is the size of hydrogen containers in cars a big problem?
8. What happened to the airship "Hindenburg"?
9. Under which conditions can hydrogen be used safely to power cars?
10. Where will the energy that is needed to produce hydrogen come from?

Activity 12, page 104: Working with words

1. fossil fuels
2. greenhouse effect
3. atmosphere
4. internal combustion engines
5. water vapour
6. CO_2
7. fuel cells
8. combined
9. hydrogen
10. containers
11. flammable
12. vehicles

Activity 13, page 104: Translation

Eine Brennstoffzelle besteht aus zwei Elektroden und einem Elektrolyten dazwischen. Wenn Sauerstoff über die eine Elektrode strömt und Wasserstoff über die andere, wird neben Wasser und Wärme auch Elektrizität erzeugt. Die Anode der Brennstoffzelle wird mit Wasserstoff versorgt, während Sauerstoff (oder Luft) über die Kathode zugeführt wird. Mit Hilfe eines Katalysators werden die Elektronen von den Wasserstoffatomen getrennt. Protonen und Elektronen gelangen über unterschiedliche Wege zur Kathode. Die Protonen wandern durch den Elektolyten. Die Elektronen stellen einen elektrischen Strom dar, der zum Antrieb eines Verbrauchers genutzt werden kann. An der Kathode vereinen sich Elektronen und Protonen und verbinden sich zusammen mit dem Sauerstoff zu Wassermolekülen.

10 Automotive Technology

Activity 1, page 107: Working with words

a)
1. Werkbank
2. Schraubstock
3. Werkzeugwagen
4. Kompressor
5. Hebebühne
6. Schweißgerät
7. Altölbehälter
8. Feuerlöscher
9. Druckmanometer
10. Diagnosezentrum
11. Wagenheber
12. Schrank
13. Waschbecken

b)
1. tool trolley
2. vice
3. diagnostic centre
4. cupboard
5. washbasin
6. pressure gauge
7. car lift
8. fire extinguisher

Activity 2, page 108: Comprehension

1. Jimmy starts his apprenticeship as a car mechanic today.
2. Mr Hendrix is busy writing job cards, when Jimmy enters the office.
3. Mr Clapton is the master mechanic of the workshop.
4. Jimmy's father has a workbench in his cellar.
5. The mechanic Eric keeps his tools in the tool trolley.

Activity 3, page 109: Working with words

a)
1. socket set
2. feeler gauge
3. rubber mallet
4. centre punch
5. strap wrench
6. grip vice pliers
7. spark plug wrench
8. side cutter
9. torque wrench
10. lever
11. rim wrench
12. ring spanner
13. wire brush
14. set of Allen keys
15. combination pliers
16. long-nose pliers
17. open-ended spanner

b)
1. Allen key
2. spark plug wrench
3. wire brush
4. torque wrench
5. feeler gauge
6. side cutter
7. centre punch
8. strap wrench
9. lever
10. rim wrench

c) Examples are:
- The tool I am describing looks like a cross. It is used when you want to take off a wheel.
  No. 11: the rim wrench
- A kind of belt is connected to an iron bar and it is used, for example, to loosen oil filters.
  No. 5: the strap wrench
- It is a special tool to tighten bolts and nuts according to standards.
  No. 9: the torque wrench.

Activity 4, page 111: Vocabulary

a) 1. Kupplung
2. Kraftfahrzeug
3. Motor
4. Federung/Aufhängung
5. Ausstattung
6. Gesetz
7. Verschmutzung
8. Einrichtung/Leichtigkeit
9. Insasse/Bewohner
10. Unfall
11. Insassen
12. Bestandteile
13. Kunde
14. Konstruktion/konstruieren
15. Sicherheit

b) 1. – c); 2. – d); 3. – c); 4. – c); 5. – b); 6. – b)

Activity 5, page 111: Understanding the text

a) 1. False. The clutch is connected to the crankshaft of the engine but it is a part of the drive train. It disconnects the gear box from the engine.
2. True. – 3. True.
4. False. Active safety refers to features of the vehicle which reduce the probability of an accident.
5. False. When engineers develop a new car they have to pay attention to many different interests and regulations, therefore, it is complicated and expensive to produce a car.
6. True. – 7. True. – 8. True.

b) 1. The five components are: the engine, the drive train, the chassis, the body, and the electrical system.
2. Active safety reduces the probability of an accident. Passive safety protects the occupants in case of an accident.
3. The brake system belongs to the component of the chassis.
4. When designing a car the engineers have to pay attention to the law, pollution, purpose of use, and to customers' wishes.
5. It is complicated to produce a car because the engineers have to pay attention to the law, pollution, safety, purpose of use, and to customers' wishes. The car is subdivided into many different sections and components. The single components have to form a unit to allow the car to move.

Activity 6, page 114: Comprehension

a) 1. During the power stroke the intake valve is closed.
2. The five components are the engine block, the crank mechanism, the timing control, the mixture formation, and the assisting equipment.
3. TDC is top dead centre. The meaning of BDC is bottom dead centre.
4. The crankshaft and the piston are connected by the connecting rod.
5. The ratio is 1:2. That means, the camshaft rotates half as often as the crankshaft.
6. The second stroke is called "compression stroke".
7. During the compression stroke the air-fuel mixture is compressed by the movement of the piston from BDC to TDC. Prior to TDC the mixture ignites.
8. The rocker shaft belongs to the section of the timing control.
9. The camshaft belongs to the timing control and the crankshaft belongs to the crank mechanism.

b) 1. – c); 2. – f); 3. – e); 4. – a); 5. – d); 6. – b)

Activity 7, page 114: Working with words

1. ignited
2. half as often
3. reciprocal
4. a) heat energy
   b) mechanical energy
5. internal combustion engines
6. connected

Activity 8, page 114: Understanding the text

a) Four strokes are necessary to carry out one operating cycle of the engine. A stroke means the movement of the piston either from TDC to BDC or from BDC to TDC. Therefore the crankshaft, which is connected to the piston by the connecting rod, turns twice to complete the full operating cycle.
The first stroke is the intake stroke. Here the piston moves from TDC to BDC. The inlet valve is open, so that a mixture of air and fuel can enter the combustion chamber.
The second stroke is the compression stroke. Here the piston moves from BDC to TDC. Both valves are closed. Due to the movement of the piston the air-fuel mixture gets compressed. The air-fuel mixture ignites either by the heat or by a spark before the TDC is reached.
The third stroke is the power stroke. Both valves are closed. The air-fuel mixture burns rapidly and expands vigorously. The power of the expanding gas forces the piston from TDC to BDC.
During the fourth stroke, which is called the exhaust stroke, the inlet valve is closed and the exhaust valve is open. The movement of the piston from BDC to TDC pushes the burned gas out of the combustion chamber.

b) Engines burn an air-fuel mixture. The generated heat energy is converted into mechanical energy. The movement of the piston in the cylinder is transmitted to a crankshaft by a connecting rod. This reciprocal movement of the piston is converted into a rotating movement of the crankshaft.
The exchange of the gas in the combustion chamber is controlled by valves.

Activity 9, page 116: Working with words

No.	English	German
1.	clutch	Kupplung
2.	gear box	Getriebe
3.	propeller shaft	Kardanwelle
4.	differential unit	Differenzial
5.	drive shafts	Antriebswellen
6.	wheels	Räder

Activity 10, page 116: Understanding the text

a) The five components of the drive train in the correct order of the power flow are: the clutch, the gear box, the propeller shaft, the differential unit, and the drive shafts.

b) 1. False. Mike is not sure, but he tried to answer.
   2. False. The clutch connects the engine to the gear box. The gear box is connected to the differential unit by the propeller shaft.
   3. True.
   4. False. The engine is a component of its own. The components of the drive train are the clutch, the gear box, the propeller shaft, the differential unit and the drive shafts.
   5. True.
   6. True.

c) 1. The main purpose of the clutch is to allow a gradual and smooth start from a position at rest. Furthermore, the clutch disconnects the engine from the gear box if we want to change gears.
   2. The prop shaft is needed on rear-wheel driven vehicles only. On front-wheel driven vehicles the gear box and the differential are built as one unit. Therefore, the prop shaft is not necessary.
   3. The prop shaft transmits the rotation from the gear box to the differential unit. The drive shafts transmit the rotation from the differential unit to the wheels.
   4. The gear box makes it possible to drive at different speed levels, from starting off, up to high speeds or driving up a hill. When reversing, the rotation is inverted inside the gear box.
   5. The power flow from the engine to the wheels takes place in the drive train.
   6. The differential unit is responsible for the adaptation of the wheel rotation in a curve.

Activity 11, page 118: Vocabulary

a) 1. Hauptbremszylinder
   2. Bremskraftverstärker
   3. Bremsscheibe
   4. Bremsklotz
   5. Bremssattel
   6. Bremsschlauch
   7. Bremsleitung
   8. Bremstrommel
   9. Bremsbacke
   10. Radbremszylinder
   11. Bremsflüssigkeit

b) 1. – c)
   2. – c)
   3. – b)
   4. – a)
   5. – c)
   6. – b)

Activity 12, page 118: Comprehension

a) 1. False. It is recommended to change brake fluid once a year.
   2. True.
   3. False. Modern cars are equipped with hydraulic brake systems. According to the law an additional mechanical brake system is also necessary.
   4. True. – 5. True. – 6. True.
   7. False. When constructing a brake system, attention has also to be paid to the maximum speed of the vehicle.
   8. False. Steam is compressible.

b) 1. Modern cars are equipped with hydraulic brake systems. According to the law an additional mechanical brake system is also necessary.

2. When constructing a brake system engineers must pay attention to the type and weight of the vehicle, the maximum speed, the layouts and the laws.

3. The main differences between the disc brake and the drum brake are:
   - The disc brake has got a better self-cleaning effect.
   - The drum brake is more affected by brake fading than the disc brake.
   - The materials of the disc brake are worn out more easily.

4. The disc brake system needs the master cylinder, the brake pipe, the brake hose, the brake calliper, the brake pads, the brake disc, and the brake fluid.

5. When the brake pedal is pressed, the brake fluid is displaced from the brake master cylinder into the wheel cylinders via brake pipes and brake hoses. This causes a movement of the pistons in the brake callipers which presses the brake pads towards the brake disc and causes friction. The function of the drum brake is quite similar.

6. In the hydraulic brake system the brake fluid is required to transmit the pressure from the master cylinder to the wheel cylinders via brake pipes and brake hoses.

7. Brake fluid is hygroscopic, it absorbs humidity from the atmosphere. If the mixture of brake fluid and water gets hot, the water evaporates and forms steam bubbles. As steam is compressible, the displacement from the master cylinder cannot be transported to the wheel cylinders directly. Therefore, it is recommended to change the brake fluid once a year.

8. The brake lining and the brake pad materials are worn out by the high temperatures caused by the force of friction. Futhermore, the brake drum expands and the gap between the brake lining and the brake drum increases. This leads to the reduction of the braking force called "brake fading".

11 Working on Metal

Activity 1, page 122: Matching exercise

Letter	English	German
a)	cutting edge	Hauptschneide
b)	clearance surface	Hauptfreifläche
c)	tip angle	Spitzenwinkel
d)	clearance angle	Freiwinkel
e)	chisel edge	Querschneide
f)	body clearance	Nebenfreifläche
g)	land	Nebenschneide
h)	chip surface	Spanfläche
i)	chamfer	Führungsfase
j)	chip flute	Spannut
k)	chisel edge angle	Querschneidenwinkel

Activity 2, page 123: Understanding technical descriptions

1. The cutting lips must be equally long, there must be a correct clearance area behind the cutting lips, the chisel-edge angle and the drill-point angle must be correctly sized.
2. The drill-point angle for normal steel is 118°.
3. The grinder must be ready. That means the face of the grinding wheel must be clean, perfectly round and right-angled with the sides of the wheel. In addition, the tool rest must be adjusted about 1 mm from the face of the wheel.
4. If the point gets hot, you have drawn the temper of the steel. You can avoid this by grinding very carefully and not let the point get too hot. You should be able to hold the point in your bare hand.
5. You must continue grinding until you have ground away the soft part of the point. Be careful and do not let the point get too hot again.

Activity 3, page 124: Finding information in a text

1. When the drill becomes shorter after repeated sharpening the web gets thicker. Thus it should be thinned to about 10% of the drill diameter.
2. You can do this by using a thin shaped grinding wheel with a thickness of half the drill diameter.
3. A too thin web may cause splitting up the web.
4. Flatter point angles reduce the danger of burrs on the underside and breakage of the drill.
5. A flat point leads to concave cutting lips which weakens the outer corners.
6. Such drill-point angles are used to reduce the tendency of flaking on the underside of brittle materials.

Activity 4, page 125: Defining technical terms

1. turning, drilling or milling
2. curved
3. surface
4. computer numerical control
5. groove
6. wedge
7. diameter
8. chisel
9. feed

Activity 5, page 126: Understanding technical descriptions

1. The main difference between up-cut milling and synchronous milling is the rotation direction in relation to the feed movement. We call it up-cut milling when the feed movement is directed against the rotation of the milling tool. In synchronous milling the rotation of the tool and the feed movement point into the same direction.
2. Both methods produce comma-shaped chips.
3. Synchronous milling produces smoother surfaces, provided the milling machine is constructed for this type of milling.
4. Before the cutting process starts the tool slides across the surface until the pressure on the chisel edge gets too strong. Then the tool starts cutting off a comma-shaped chip until the tooth leaves the workpiece. Each tooth leaves a wavy mark in the surface.
5. Up-cut milling is an advantage when you have a hard surface. It is also an advantage when your milling machine does not have a ballscrew in the table drive, because with a normal threaded spindle there is no tendency of wedging the workpiece under the tool in up-cut milling.

Activity 6, page 126: Giving explanations

1. Up-cut milling: Feed movement and rotation direction point into the opposite direction.
2. Infeed: It describes how thick the layer is which you cut off in mm.
3. Synchronous milling: Feed movement and rotation direction point into the same direction.
4. Feed direction: Direction into which the work piece moves
5. Chip: The comma-shaped piece of metal which is cut off by the tool.
6. Smooth surface: A surface without any waves or grooves
7. Diameter: The line through a circle which goes exactly through the middle from one side to the other.
8. Cone: A geometrical body that has a circular base and a point as the top
9. Cylinder: A geometrical body that has a circular base and a circular cover.
10. Lip clearance area: The area that is ground away behind the cutting edge of a tool.

Activity 7, page 126: Describing a technical process

In the cylindrical milling process the axis of the milling tool and the surface of the workpiece are parallel to each other. The feed direction can either be in or against the rotation direction of the milling tool. Usually there is only one tooth in operation.
In face milling the tool axis is vertical in relation to the surface of the workpiece. There are always more than one tooth in operation and up-cut milling and down-cut milling can be found at the same time. Face milling causes a smoother running and a high cutting performance.

Activity 8, page 127: Translation

In milling the chip forming process is caused by a circular movement of the milling tool and a straight feed movement and depth setting performed by the workpiece. The relation between feed movement and cutting movement is very important for the chip forming process. If feed movement and cutting movement are directed towards each other, it is called up-cut milling. If they are directed in the same direction, it is called synchronous milling

Activity 9, page 128: Working with words

1. chip
2. chisel edge
3. geometrically defined
4. circular
5. cross slide
6. chuck
7. lathe
8. shape
9. revolutions (per minute)
10. diameter
11. feed
12. depth setting
13. surface
14. cylindrical
15. cone
16. thread

Activity 10, page 128: Asking questions and finding answers

Question	Answer
What are the apprentices doing?	They are producing a workpiece.
What is the apprentice on the left doing?	He is measuring the length of the workpiece.
What are both apprentices wearing to protect their eyes?	They are wearing goggles.
Where are both apprentices standing?	They are standing behind a lathe.
What is the student on the left holding in his hands?	He is holding a vernier calliper in his hands.
What is lying on the top slide?	There are a lot of metal chips lying on the top slide.

12 Electrical Engineering

Activity 1, page 132: Working with measuring instruments

a) 1. analog multimeter
2. frequency counter
3. oscilloscope
4. energy meter
5. function generator
6. voltage tester
7. clamp ammeter
8. digital multimeter

b) 1. With an analog multimeter you can measure current, voltage, resistance, and check continuity.
2. With a frequency counter you can count the frequency of a signal.
3. With an oscilloscope you can display a signal and measure its voltage as well as time and frequency of the signal.
4. With an energy meter you can measure energy consumption.
5. With a function generator you can generate different kinds of signals like sinus or rectangle.
6. With a voltage tester you can check if a wire is live or not.
7. With a clamp ammeter you can measure electric current without breaking the circuit.
8. With a digital multimeter you can measure current, voltage, resistance, frequency, temperature, and transistor gain. Moreover, you can test the function of diodes, and check continuity.

Activity 2, page 134: Parts of a multimeter

1. – b); 2. – e); 3. – f); 4. – d); 5. – a); 6. – c)

Activity 3, page 134: Dialogue

Question	Answer
Is it a digital multimeter?	Yes, it is.
What can it measure?	It can measure current, voltage, resistance, and it can test transistors and diodes.
What kind of battery does it need?	It needs a standard 9-volt battery.
What does the multimeter weigh?	It weighs approximately 340 grams including battery and holster.
Has it got an autorange function?	No, it does not have an autorange function.
What kind of display does it have?	It has a 3 ½ digit LCD display.
What's its input impedance?	When measuring DC the input impedance is 1 MΩ and with AC it is 450 kΩ.
Has it got overload protection?	Yes, the overload protection is 600 volts DC and 600 volts AC rms.

Activity 4, page 135: Matching exercise

a) and b)

1. squirrel-cage motor – machine tools, blowers, electrical drives in agriculture
2. DC motor – machine tools
3. capacitor motor – power tools, household appliances
4. shaded-pole motor – control units (Schaltwerke, e.g. in dish washers), turntables, heater, blowers, spin dryers (Wäscheschleudern)
5. linear motor – maglev (magnetic levitation) trains (Transrapid)
6. slip ring motor – engines that must start under full load, e.g. cranes

Activity 5, page 136: Comprehension

1.

German	English
Klemmbrett	connecting terminal plate
Ständerblechpaket	stator lamination pack
Ständerwicklung	stator winding
Lager	bearing
Welle	shaft
Kurzschlussring	rotor end rings
Gehäuse	casing
Läuferblechpaket	rotor lamination pack
Lüfter	cooling fan

2. The rotation speed of the magnetic field in the stator and the rotation speed of the rotor are not equal. The latter lags behind. The rotating magnetic field in the stator induces an electric current in the bars of the squirrel-cage of the rotor. As a result the bars also become magnetic and try to follow the rotation of the magnetic field in the stator. In this way the rotor starts turning.

3.

Advantages	Use	Parts of the stator	Parts of the rotor
robust	machine tools	casing	shaft
cheap	blower fans in agriculture	stator lamination pack	rotor lamination pack
maintenance-free		stator winding	squirrel-cage

Activity 6, page 138: Comprehension

1. James Collins has got another job for Mark and Phil to do before they can return to the company.
2. Mark thinks mobile phones are basically toys for adults but he admits that they can be quite useful in certain situations.
3. A BTS is the technical centre of each cell. It is responsible for receiving and sending all the signals that are necessary to communicate via mobile phone.
4. It is the Home MSC (Mobile Switching Centre).
5. A handover (also called "hand off") takes place whenever a subscriber moves to an adjacent cell while a call is in progress. In this case the BTS of the new cell becomes responsible for handling the call.
6. Individual answer.
7. Due to the drawing only the MSCs can establish a connection between two subscribers. That means the calling subscriber gets in contact with the BTS of "his" cell. The BTS routes the call via BSC and TCE to the MSC which is responsible for the call. The MSC finds the Home MSC of the person to be called and thus gets the information whether he/she is available and where he or she is. If the person is available, the system establishes the call. Otherwise the calling subscriber gets a message that the person he/she is calling is not available.

Activity 7, page 142: Talking about electronic components

a) From left to right: Integrated Circuit (IC) – resistor – voltage regulator – (power) transistor – SMD transistor

b) The first figure (3.9 k or 15 k) describes the resistance value, the second informs about the maximum power consumption (e.g. 0.5 W) and the third indicates the tolerance of the value of the resistance (e.g. +/– 5 %).

c)

German	**English**
Widerstand	resistor
Transistor	transistor
Diode	diode
Relais	relay
Tranformator	transformer
Leuchtdiode	LED (light emitting diode)
Potentiometer	potentiometer
Kondensator	capacitor
Elektrolytkondensator	electrolytic capacitor
Spule	coil
Fotowiderstand	LDR (light dependent resistor)
Heißleiter	NTC resistor (thermal resistor)
Kaltleiter	PTC resistor
Varistor	varistor (VDR– voltage dependent resitor)

German	English
Operationsverstärker	op-amp
Digitale Gatter	digital gates
Zähler	counter
Schieberegister	shift register
Lampe	lamp
Schalter	switch
IC	integrated circuit
Fototransistor	photo transistor
Kapazitätsdiode	tuning diode, varactor diode
Quarz	quartz crystal
Thyristor	thyristor

d) Individual answers, e.g.:

KATING: Hello, Eurotechnologies, Michael Kating speaking. Can I help you?

GRANGER: Good morning Mr Kating. This is Peter Granger, London Electronics Ltd. I would like to talk to you about your latest order.

KATING: Good morning Mr Granger. What about it?

GRANGER: Unfortunately, we can't deliver some of the components you ordered. We are sold out with the …

Activity 8, page 142: Transistors

1. silicon
2. three
3. emitter
4. controlled
5. input
6. semi-conducting
7. electric field
8. amplifiers

Activity 9, page 143: Defining resistors

a)
1. blue/grey/yellow/silver → 680 kΩ ± 10%
2. brown/black/black/gold → 10 Ω ± 5%
3. orange/green/red/red → 3500 Ω ± 2%
4. yellow/violet/orange/silver → 47 kΩ ± 10%
5. white/brown/brown/gold → 910 Ω ± 5%

b)
a) 120 Ω → brown/red/brown
b) 4.7 MΩ → yellow/violet/green
c) 68 Ω → blue/grey/black
d) 33 kΩ → orange/orange/orange
e) 820 kΩ → grey/red/yellow
f) 560 Ω → green/blue/brown
g) 1000 Ω → brown/black/red

13 Automotive Electric

Activity 1, page 147: Talking about the electrical system

a)

English	German
clock	Zeituhr
horn	Hupe
windscreen wiper	Scheibenwischer
interior light	Innenbeleuchtung
main beam	Fernlicht
dipped beam	Abblendlicht
clearance lamp	Stand-/ Begrenzungslicht

English	German
fog light front	Nebelscheinwerfer
fog light rear	Nebelschlussleuchte
reverse lamps	Rückfahrscheinwerfer
break light	Bremslicht
indicator light	Blinklicht
rear window defroster	Heckscheibenheizung
starter motor	Starter/Anlasser

b) 2 fog lights, fog light rear, dipped beam left and right, 4 clearence lamps, ignition, heater

c)

2 fog lights front	110 W
fog light rear	21 W
dipped beam left and right	110 W
4 clearance lamps	40 W
ignition	100 W
heater	300 W
total	681 W

d) Examples are:

1. In contemporary motor vehicles one can find the power supply-, safety- and security systems, and the comfort-board system and the electronic controlled fuel systems.
2. When the engine is off, the hazard warning light gets the power from the car battery.
3. ECU stands for Electrical Control Unit which is a kind of on-board computer.
4. The alternator and the car battery belong to the supply system.
5. When many electrical devices are switched on and the car is used mostly for short distances, the power supply might not be enough to recharge the car battery.
6. The starter motor is supplied with electrical power by the car battery.
7. Electronic controlled fuel systems are essential to reduce emissions.
8. Yes. Increasing numbers of electrical devices require an increasing amount of electricity.

Activity 2 page 149: Comprehension

a) 1. The light is not only to see, it is also to be seen.
   2. All lights should be checked before driving the vehicle.
   3. The inclination of the headlight should be checked once a year.
   4. While in use H 4-lamps get very hot.
   5. A H 4-lamp is a lamp with two wires, one for the main beam and one for the dipped beam.

b) Possible answer:
The advantage of the asymmetrical dipped beam is the illumination of the side of the road. Therefore pedestrians who are walking on the side of the road or animals can be seen earlier.

c) Clearance lamps around the vehicle are necessary to make the contours visible in the darkness.

d) 1. The function of the head light is to illuminate the road surface and the side of the road.
   2. Additionally a fog light can be fitted in the front of a car. They always have to be mounted in pairs.
   3. Due to the density of today's traffic the dipped beam is most often used for driving.
   4. The indicator lamps are to indicate intended manoeuvres to other road users.
   5. The degree of illumination of the road surface depends on the type of headlight. It also depends on the beam as well as on the inclination setting.

Activity 3, page 151: Talking about the airbag

a) 1. The airbag belongs to the interior safety zone.
   2. The very first airbags were fitted in the steering wheel.
   3. The first production car was equipped with an airbag in the year 1981.
   4. It takes 30 milliseconds for an airbag to deploy.
   5. The driver's airbag prevents the driver's head and upper body from impacting the steering wheel.
   6. Passenger cars are equipped with front airbags, side airbags, window airbags and other airbags.
   7. The interior safety zone reduces the risk of injury in the interior of the passenger cell. Sometimes it is a combination of different safety systems such as a restraint system and impact-protection measures.
   8. Activated by a crash, the sensor triggers the inflator to produce an electric spark that ignites the sodium azide, which rapidly produces gas that passes through a filter and inflates the airbag.
   9. The airbag deflates immediately so the driver is able to see out of the windscreen in case further reactions are necessary.
   10. After the crash sensor gets activated it triggers the inflator to produce an electrical spark that ignites the sodium azide.
   11. After the sodium azide is ignited it produces mainly nitrogen and carbon dioxide.
   12. The gas of the airbag is discharged into the atmosphere via outlet openings facing away from the occupant's side.

b) Phase one: When the accident starts, the crash sensor triggers the inflator.

Phase two: After about 15 milliseconds the sodium azide is ignited and the resulting gas starts to fill up the airbag.

Phase three: The airbag is fully inflated. 45 milliseconds after the start of the accident, the driver's upper body moves forwards.

Phase four: 80 milliseconds have elapsed when the driver's head and the upper body make contact with the airbag.

Phase five: Only 150 milliseconds after the start of the accident the airbag is deflated and the driver is able to see out of the windscreen again.

c)
1. False. The airbag prevents the driver's head and upper body from impacting the steering wheel. The airbag is a part of the interior safety zone. Therefore it reduces the risk of injury in the interior of the passenger cell.
2. True.
3. True.
4. False. As the impact continues and the airbag fully inflates, it deflates immediately so the driver is able to see out of the windscreen in case further reactions are necessary.
5. True.
6. False. According to accident research the airbag has saved thousands of lives all over the world.
7. True.
8. True.
9. True.
10. False. The gas from the airbag is discharged to atmosphere via outlet openings facing away from the occupant's side so they do not inhale them.
11. True.